We're Off...
to
White Sands
National Monument, NM

Nos Vamos...

al

Monumento Nacional de

White Sands (Arenas Blancas),

Nuevo Méjico

Georgette Baker

Photographs by Georgette Baker

Translation by Georgette Baker

Email : jarjetb@writeme.com
http://www.cantemosco.com

Lizard and beetle photographs purchased from istock 2016

This is the United States of America.

Esto es Los Estados Unidos de América.

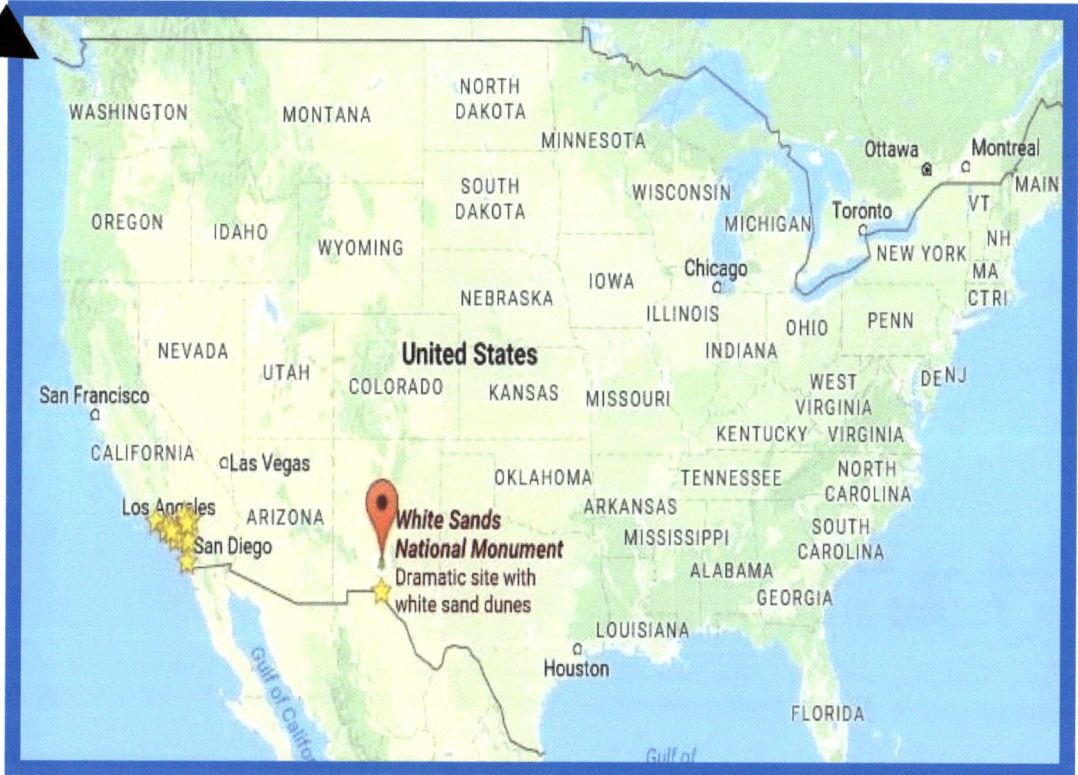

White Sands National Monument is located in the state of New Mexico.

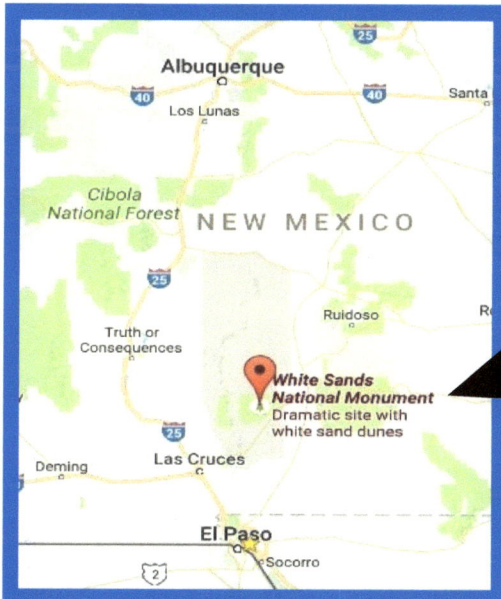

El Monument Nacional White Sands está en el estado de Nuevo Méjico.

White Sands National Monument is

275 miles of pure white sand,

the largest gypsum dunes in the world!

El Monumento Nacional White Sands es compuesto de

275 millas de arena de yeso blanco.

¡Las dunas de yeso más grandes del mundo!

How were the dunes formed?

It started with a mountain full of the mineral gypsum.

When rain pelted down it broke up the soft mineral.

Wind blew the pieces around breaking them down further.

¿Cómo se formaron las dunas?

Comenzó con una montaña de mineral de yeso que fué erosionada por la caída de fuertes lluvias, formando partículas de mineral blando. Arrastradas, por el viento, estas partículas de yeso se fragmentaron aún más.

Gypsum is so fragile that it is easily broken down into sand-size grains. The gypsum sand is moved by the winds creating great dunes. This process continues even today.

El yeso es tan frágil que fácilmente es reducido en tamaño granos de arena. La arena de yeso es movida por el viento creando las grandes dunas . Este proceso contunúa aún hoy en dia.

Gypsum is used as a fertilizer, in plaster and

black-board chalk.

Este es el mismo yeso (gypsum) que se utiliza en

fertilizante, en paredes y en tiza.

There is also life in these gypsum dunes.

Little Rose, *Rosita*
Gypsum Centaury

En estas dunas de yeso también hay vida.

Torrey's Jointfir, related to the pine tree, was used by Mescalero Apache Indians to treat eye infections.

Se encuentra un arbusto llamado Torrey's Joint-fir que es relacionado con el árbol de pino. Este arbusto fue utilizado por los indios Apache Mescaleros para tratar infecciones de los ojos.

The Soaptree Yucca is another plant found in this area.

Inside its trunk is a soapy substance used as soap.

La Yucca Elata es otra planta que se encuentra en esta área. Dentro de su tronco hay una sustancia jabonosa que se utiliza como jabón.

Alkali Sacaton is a grass whose seeds provide food for birds and rodents.

Alkali Sacaton es una hierba cuyas semillas proporcionan alimento para aves y roedores..

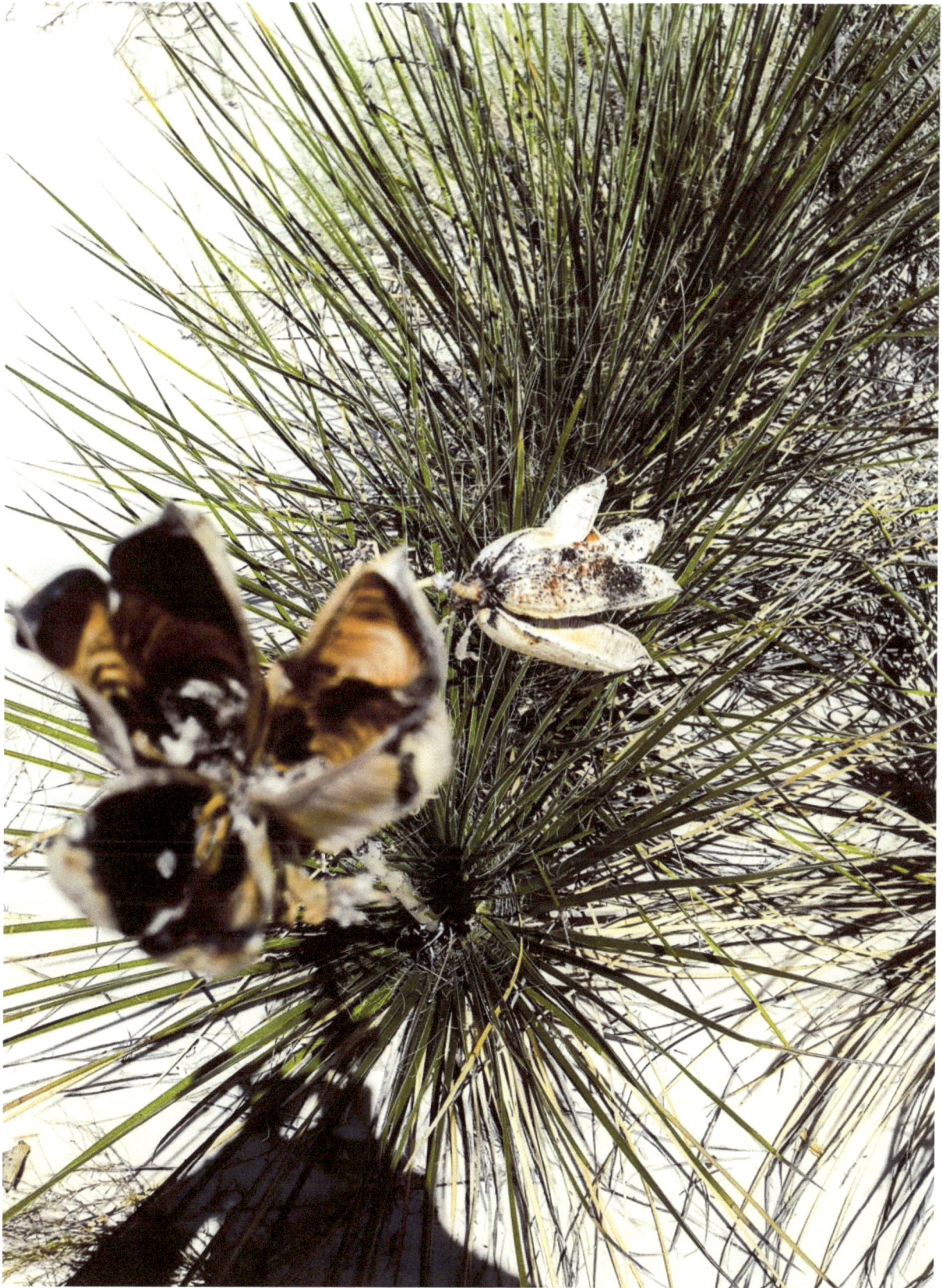

Also found are animals like the earless lizard, the Apache pocket mouse and the fox. Their coats are much lighter, almost light grey or white..

También se encuentran aimales como el lagarto sin orejas y el ratón Apache de bolsillo y el zorro. Sus pieles son muy claras, casi gris o blanco.

A lighter color coat and skin reflects light keeping the animals cooler and helping them hide from predators.

El color claro en estos animales ayuda a que se refleje la luz, y así se mantienen más frescos. Además, les sirve de camuflaje para ocultarse de los depredadores .

.

Animal footprints in the sand.

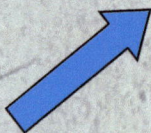

Huellas de animales en la arena.

The Darkling Beetle, one of the easier creatures to spot on the dunes, wanders around mostly at night.

El escarabajo Darkling, es una de las criaturas más fácil de ver en las dunas, se pasea por la noche.

Ramps make parts of the dunes accessible to all.

Rampas hacen partes de las dunas accesible a todos.

Informative signs give visitors an opportunity to learn

about the flora and fauna of the dunes.

Cyanobacteria

In the interdunal areas (low areas between dunes), you will see a bumpy, raised surface covering the sand. What you are looking at is cyanobacteria—a woven mat of organisms living on the soil surface.

The cyanobacteria adds nutrients to the sand, allowing plants to grow. It also holds rainwater like a sponge and slows erosion. The crust is very fragile and can be damaged if you walk on it. So be careful not to bust the crust—plants need it to survive!

Señas con información dan , a los visitants, la oportunidad

de aprender sobre la flora y la fauna de las dunas.

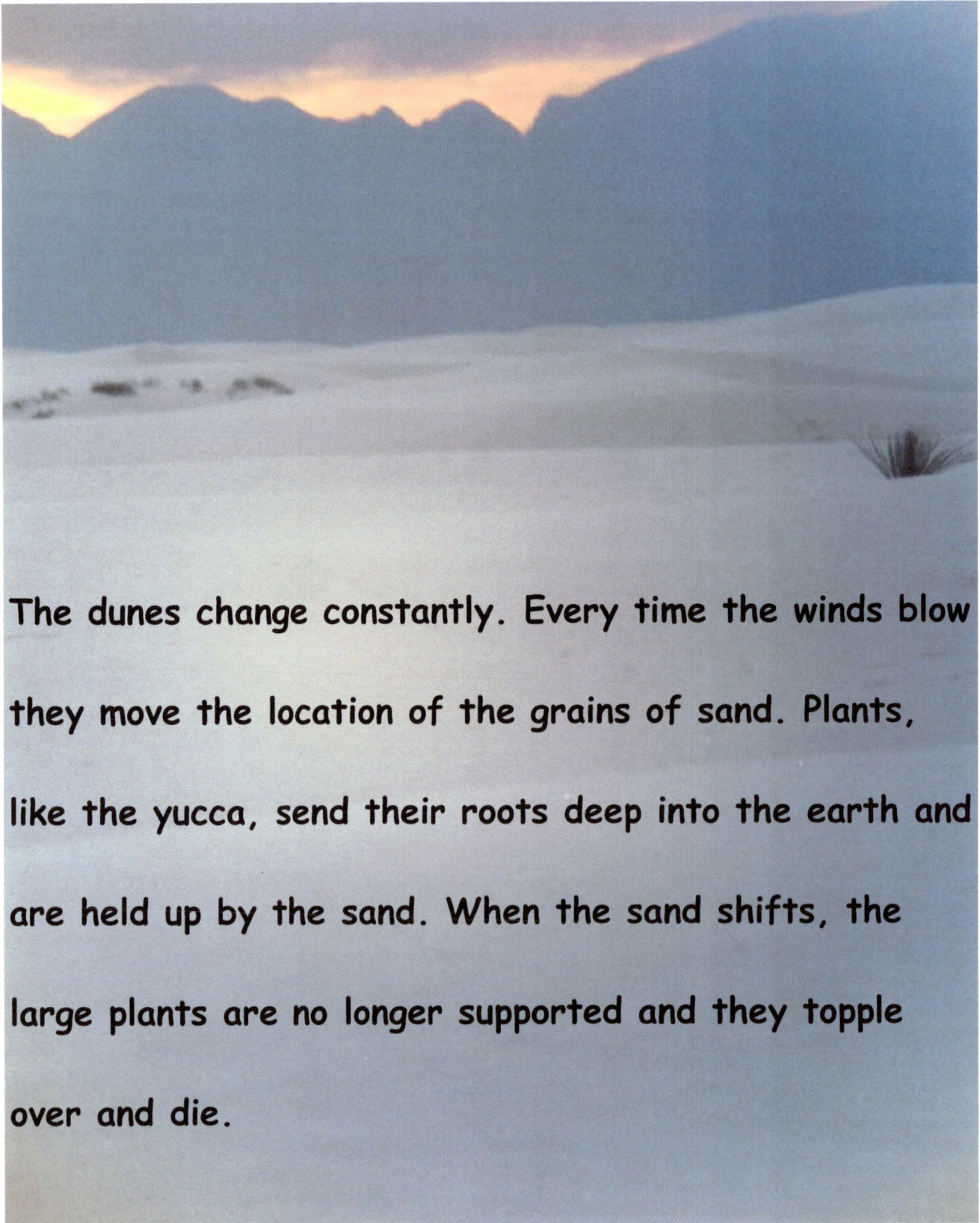

The dunes change constantly. Every time the winds blow

they move the location of the grains of sand. Plants,

like the yucca, send their roots deep into the earth and

are held up by the sand. When the sand shifts, the

large plants are no longer supported and they topple

over and die.

Las dunas cambian constantemente, cada vez que sopla el

viento la arena cambia de lugar. Las plantas , como la yucca,

deben agarrarse con profundas raíces y son apoyadas por la

arena. Cuando se desplaza la arena, las grandes plantas ya

no estan apoyadas, se caen y se mueren.

President Herbert Hoover declared White Sands a

National Monument in 1933.

El Presidente Herbert Hoover declaró a White Sands un

monumento nacional en 1933.

White Sands National Monument is a place to explore,

enjoy as a family and much more.

El Monumento Nacional White Sands es un lugar para

explorar, disfrutar en familia y mucho más.

BOOKS AND CD'S WRITTEN BY GEORGETTE BAKER available on amazon.com   email: bakergeorgette@yahoo

Http://www.cantemosco.com   Http://www.simplespanishsongs.com

- Aesop's Fables/Las Fabulas...
- Aluminum Castles
- Andi y la Mina de Oro
- Andy and the Gold Mine
- CANCIONES INFANTILES...
- Canciones Infantiles/Spanish...
- Castillos de Aluminio
- Children's Author Presentation Handbook
- Cuentos y Canciones/ Stories...
- Funics! Phonemic Awareness...
- Hallacas Venezolanas
- Las Fábulas de Ésopo
- Multicultural Stories
- Multicultural Stories/Cuentos...
- Patriotic American...
- Periquito
- Sandwiched
- Settle Down Sounds
- Sonidos Serenos
- TAGALOG Made Easy
- The Baby Manual
- We're Off to the Galapagos
- WE're Off...to Australia's Great...
- We're Off...to Kenya
- We're Off...to Learn Some...
- We're Off...to Mo'orea
- We're Off...to Peru

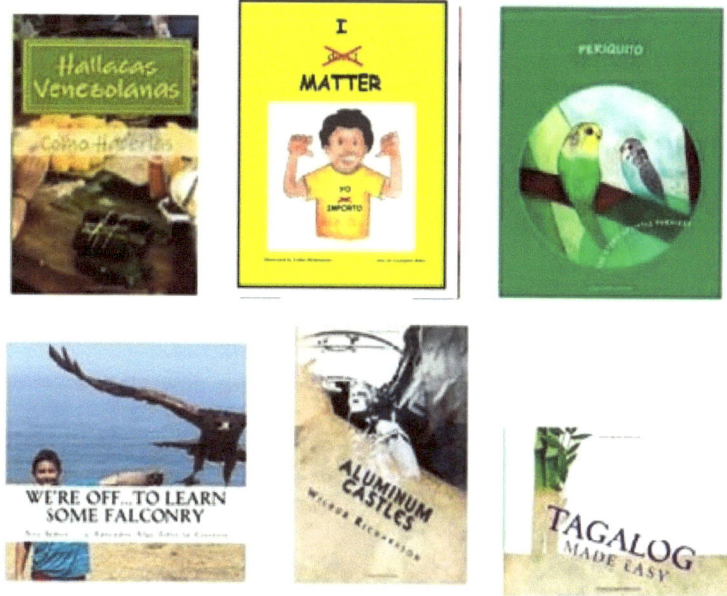

909-239-2735 CANTEMOS BILINGUAL CDS AND BOOKS

Cuentos y Canciones/ Stories and Songs

Canciones Infantiles/ Spanish Songs for Kids

Las Fabulas de Esopo/ Aesop's Fables

Funemic Awareness

Settle Down Sounds

Patriotic American Songs

Multicultural Stories/ Cuentos Multiculturales

Contemos Chiquitos

Contemos Chiquitos #2

WE'RE OFF TO...BILINGUAL SERIES $12.95 EACH

AUSTRALIA- GREAT BARRIER REEF   PERU   MOOREA   KENYA   GALAPAGOS

www.cantemosco.com   Amazon.com Tel 909-239-2735   email: bakergeorgette@yahoo.com

www.ingramcontent.com/pod-product-compliance
Lightning Source LLC
Chambersburg PA
CBHW060855270326
41934CB00002B/148